WE ARE LIFE

PETER GRIFFITHS

Peter Griffiths/Lifeskills Bookshop Pty Ltd
www.petergriffithsauthor.com

Cover design by Chris Hildenbrand
Cover image by Getty Images
Typeset in Goudy Old Style 9 & 12 pt/Sylfaen 12 & 18 pt
Printed and bound in Australia by IngramSpark
Prepared for publication by The Erudite Pen

A catalogue record for this book is available from the National Library of Australia

We Are Life: Peter Griffiths ~ 1st ed.
ISBN 9780648943600

Dedication

This book is dedicated to my wife Jenny who has always encouraged me in my writing, even in the times when I spent more time talking about it rather than actually doing it. But like pregnancy and birth, this book came together in its own good time, and I am rather proud of it.

Peter Griffiths

Contents

Preface

Some seventy-five years ago, I was born into a world very different to the one that I live in today. It was 1945. The Second World War had just finished, and there was a sense of relief and optimism in the air as people set about rebuilding their lives and relationships. For many it was a fresh beginning, and my parents started from scratch as share farmers in Southern Queensland's Mary Valley just a few months before I was born.

We lived on a relatively isolated farm without electricity or telephone, which was pretty well normal for rural areas at that time. But it was a beautiful place. The old farmhouse was set on top of a ridge with mountains and valleys all around. There was also still a significant amount of rainforest on the property. A visit to the nearest town while my parents did the monthly shopping was a big adventure. Other than that, I spent the first five years of my life wandering around our farm by myself as there were no other children within walking distance.

I don't remember much of my very early years; however, as a toddler, I do have one vivid memory of Dad picking me up and sitting me on the back of one of the draft horses he used when ploughing the farm. The memory I have of this is it was just like sitting on the kitchen table as the horse's back was so broad that my legs just stuck straight out.

The first five years before I started school had a very formative effect on me. They gave me absolutely no idea how to mix and play with other children. However, I did develop an affinity with the natural world and became very self-reliant (many years later my mother said it was a wonder I was not taken by a python as I wandered around the farm alone).

My understanding of school was that it was somewhere that you just had to go until you were sixteen. So at age sixteen I left school and took up the first apprenticeship that I could find, which happened to be as a motor mechanic. By the time I was nineteen, the urge to see what life was like outside of a country town had become strong enough for me to set out and find my own way in the world.

Fast-forward eighteen months to when I met an interesting young lady in Sydney. While my conversation skills were still very underdeveloped, some of our chats awoke a part of my mind that I had not been using up until then. I remember one conversation in particular when she made the comment, 'If we can inherit instincts, why can't we inherit memory.' This comment opened my mind to a much wider perspective of what life might be, and that wider view has stayed with me ever since.

But let me explain how this book came into being. At various times over the last fifty years or so, I had jotted down notes after receiving flashes of insight into the nature of life on earth, and beyond. After recently sorting through them, I found literally hundreds of individual notes covering a wide range of thoughts and insights that must have seemed relevant to me at the time.

I had not looked at any of these jottings since they were first written down, but as I read through them, I became aware that many had interrelated themes and ideas. The more I read over them, the more interested I became in the comments and ideas they contained. The story that follows just grew from there.

The Water Dowser

To start at what I think was the beginning, I need to go back to the early 1970s. As a young man back then, there was a period when I was between employment and had time on my hands. With no particular commitments and even less spending money, a short camping trip to a nearby rural area seemed like a good idea. The next afternoon, I arrived in a quiet and picturesque country town and started asking around if there was somewhere that I could set up my tent.

I was soon directed to a local farmer who operated a small camping ground in a corner of his farm. He rented these camping sites out by the night. While I was busy erecting my tent, I struck up a conversation with this farmer. When I mentioned that I enjoyed a bit of amateur prospecting his face lit up, and he offered to show me a patch of red jasper that was not far from his farm.

Early the next morning with the farmer as my guide, we started out. Even though he was much older than me, my guide soon set a brisk pace through the beautiful but rugged countryside. After we had been walking for over an hour, my guide showed no sign of slowing down. I suggested that I'd like to stop for a few minutes so I could get my water bottle from my pack. My guide pointed to a fallen log nearby, and we sat down on the log for a breather.

As I slowly sipped the water in an effort to rest a little longer, my guide said, 'Let me show you something.' With that he stood up and walked over to a small tree growing nearby. My guide then snapped a green branch from the tree and proceeded to trim it with a pocketknife until he had a Y-shaped twig. He grasped the twig with one arm of the Y in each hand. With the longer base of the Y pointing out in front of him, he said, 'Now watch this.'

The farmer then began to walk slowly along with the twig held parallel to the ground and out in front of him. Before he had taken a dozen steps, the forward-pointing end of the twig began to quiver a little and then twist and point down to the ground. As he continued to move slowly forward, the tip of the twig began to lift until it was again parallel with the ground. The farmer scraped his boot on the ground to mark the spot where the downward indication had been strongest. He then turned towards me a said, 'My father taught me how to do this, and it's called dowsing. It's something I've been doing for as long as I can remember. When the end of the twig pulls down, it indicates that there's water moving underground at that spot. For many years now I've been helping other farmers around the district to find the most likely spots to sink a well or a bore. Would you like to try it?'

He showed me how to hold the forked twig, with the fingers of each hand curled around an arm of the Y. My thumbs pressed forward along each arm towards the longer base. Holding the forked twig out in front of me as I had been shown, I then walked over the same ground that he had recently walked over. Even though I walked directly over my guide's mark on the ground, there was no feeling or any sign of movement from the twig.

I turned around and walked slowly back over the mark, but there was still absolutely no reaction from the twig. So I moved to hand it back to my companion. He didn't take the twig but after a short deliberation he said, 'Try it again but this time we'll do something different.'

With that the farmer stood beside me, put his right hand on my left shoulder and said, 'Let's try it now.' Together we walked back towards the mark with his hand resting on my shoulder. As we neared the mark, to my surprise, I felt the twig begin to twist downwards as I had seen it do in my guide's hands. The tip of the twig pulled down strongly over the mark on the ground. As we moved past it, the pulling-down effect eased, and the twig returned to the horizontal position.

The farmer removed his hand from my shoulder and walked back to the log. He said, 'Now try it again by yourself.' I ambled back towards the mark, holding the twig as I had done the first time. This time the twig pulled down strongly, just as it did when my guide's hand was on my shoulder. I was now dowsing on my own.

For the next ten minutes or so, I experimented with my new-found skill and even found a new spot a little further on where I got another reading. In my mind I was trying to understand how this was happening and what sort of force was causing the strong downward movement of the twig. The only thought that I could come up with was that I was somehow subconsciously twisting the twig myself.

I then tried holding the twig as tightly and as parallel to the ground as I could while I again moved towards the mark on the ground. As I moved closer, I felt the twig pull downwards so redoubled my effort to hold it as tightly and as level as I could. As I continued to move closer to the mark, I felt the pulling-down effect getting stronger. Then all of a sudden the twig twisted downwards over the mark. As I relaxed my grip and looked down at my hands, I was amazed to see there were indentations in my palms. I really had been holding it tightly! The core of the twig was still fresh and sappy. It had actually torn away internally from the bark. This had allowed the twig to twist inside the bark while I still held the outer bark firmly in my hands. The very fact that the green-stick dowsing rod twisted inside the bark but still pointed downwards while I steadily held the outer bark indicated that I was not subconsciously twisting the twig. Instead, some other energy that I could not comprehend was at work.

We moved on, and I collected some nice specimens of red Jasper. But over the subsequent weeks and months, I kept thinking about my dowsing experience. Initially, the wonder was that the dowsing process was able to signal the presence of moving water. However, over time the aspect of the dowsing experience that intrigued me more was that my guide had been able to impart the dowsing ability to me simply by putting his hand on my shoulder as we walked together through the experience.

I never did meet up with the farmer again. Even though he would be long gone now, I still clearly remember dowsing for water with him some fifty years ago. I know there was some form of energy in action that day. While we do not yet know how to measure it, or even clearly define it, it seems that we are able tap into it using a dowsing tool.

Since then I have become more aware that there are still many things in this world that we do not yet understand. With that realisation, I have tried to keep an open mind about the world around me and how it works. It may not even have been water that we were sensing, given that various forms of dowsing have been used around the world to seek out all manner of things. But some form of energy was working through me that day. This inexplicable energy caused the twig to tear away internally from its outer layer of bark and twist strongly downwards. It did this consistently at the same place, time and again.

During the years that followed, the more immediate needs of making a living and raising a family took precedence. My dowsing experience gradually became little more than a memory. But every now and then over the years, I would have a sudden flash of insight into something. I instinctively knew these insights were somehow related to my dowsing experience and how the hand on my shoulder had made all the difference.

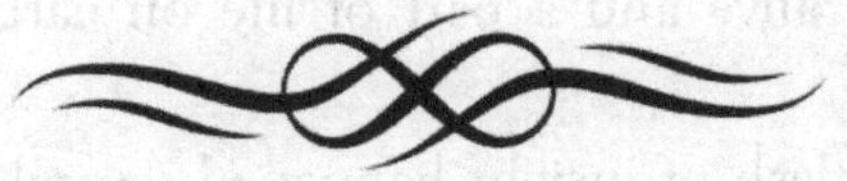

A Retirement Project

My sudden flashes of insight were few and far between in the years immediately after the dowsing experience. I had never thought to make any note of them. This was until an extremely vivid flash of awareness made a remarkable impression on me. From then on, I resolved to make a note about any significant perceptions or ideas as they occurred.

The awareness that I refer to happened on a warm, lazy day where I must have been daydreaming. I suddenly saw in my mind the silhouette of a large tree, black against a bright background. Although I did not hear any words, I was fully alert in an instant. The inference of the silhouette was that this tree was just as alive as I was, but because it did not have a heart to drive its circulation, it lived at an entirely different pace and in an entirely different way to me. However, we were each just as much alive and a part of life on earth as the other.

That flash of insight happened several years after the dowsing experience. While I have not had such a visual or intense experience since, I continued to have these occasional flashes over the years that followed. Whenever these occurred, sometimes in clusters and sometimes years apart, I would make a note of it. These are the same notes that I have recently been re-reading and putting into context.

A few years ago I made the decision to retire from the workforce and to step back from the demands of a regimented day-to-day working life. The idea was that this would allow me the time and freedom to just enjoy each day. I was pleasantly surprised at how quickly I adjusted to the pace and opportunities that retirement allowed. Over the years I have learnt that every age has its advantages. Especially once you develop the confidence that will allow you to enjoy the present and be positive about life.

With time now on my hands, I started working through the backlog of projects that I'd been continually deferring. The first of these projects was to get rid of clutter by going through our home and clearing out all the things we were no longer using.

I came up with what I thought was a good plan, where I would take everything out of a storage area and then sort through all of the items individually. After sorting, only items that had been used in the past two years or items that had a strong and still-relevant sentimental value would be returned to the storage area. Any items that did not fall into these two categories would be given away or otherwise disposed of.

While this seemed to be a good plan, it soon proved not as easy as I thought, and I ended up with a third category. This third category consisted of items that did not fit the criteria to be returned to the cupboard, but I was still finding it very difficult to dispose of them.

The more troublesome of the items in this third category were the old jotted notes on the ideas and flashes of insight I referred to earlier. The notes themselves had been haphazardly stored throughout various old notebooks, and some were also stored loosely in folders and a shoebox. Many worthy insights had been hurriedly jotted down at the time they occurred. Some insights were so cryptic or lacking in context that I had no idea what the original thought had been, so these had to be discarded.

However, once I'd gathered all remaining notes together, hundreds were legible and covered a wide range of subjects. This really surprised me.

Over the many years that I had been scribbling down my insights, I had never reviewed them. So when deciding what to do with them, I sat down and read each one. Over the next few months I read, reread and sorted the jumble of old notes into subject matter. As I did so, I noticed that many of the ideas and thoughts fit together, much like a jigsaw would fit together. As more pieces fell into place, the easier it was to see and understand the story coming together out of the various insights.

With growing interest, I began to read more widely on the subjects that were mentioned in the notes. That way, I would have a better understanding of them. Every now and then as I read and researched, I would come across something that I instinctively felt to be true. So I would make a note of that as well. Over time, as the ideas connected together and more pieces fell into place, the easier it was to visualise the story coming into focus out of this jigsaw of thoughts and ideas. Only recently, what seems to be the final piece has fallen into place.

During review, two notes in particular made a strong impression on me. Both of these struck me as being relevant and important to this undertaking, which was finding a use or purpose for the notes I had made over so many years.

The first of these two was very short, and it simply read: 'Insight and wisdom will come through you, not of you.'

The second, even though it had been jotted down some forty years earlier, gave me the idea of what I may be able to do with these notes. It read: 'You can talk to people across the years and across the generations, even though you may never meet them, simply by writing a book.'

With a couple of hundred notes on hand, covering a wide range of thoughts and ideas, now seemed to be a good time to try my hand at writing.

Over a period of about twelve months, the story that follows gradually arose out of the random collection of insights. These various insights fit together, each one into its correct place, to tell what I think is a unique and unexpected story.

When the story had basically settled into its final shape, the themes were so different to any concepts or ideas that I had formerly consciously held. I found myself thinking that this whole story did seem to fit in with the note that suggested insight and wisdom comes through you and is not necessarily of you.

The following chapters are based on the original collection of notes. The order and context of the ideas are in the order that allowed their subject matter to fall into place easily and naturally. The premise of the story is that the origin of all life is the *life energy* itself. This is a naturally occurring energy that exists throughout our solar system and throughout the universe.

When I re-read and collated these notes it became clear that many of them referred to different aspects of this same life energy, and also to the life force, but referred to them by different names at different times. These terms ranged from Mother Nature, the Universal Mind, Infinite Intelligence, the Soul and the Universal Life Force. There was also one note that referred to life energy as God within, inferring that the god within is the same deity that many of the monotheistic religions refer to as God.

For the sake of consistency, I will mostly use the term life force in the story that follows. However, there are some instances where I use the term referred to in the original note if it better suits the subject being described. To my mind, the term life force is generally inclusive of the properties of the other terms used in the original insights.

The story you are about to read gives a view of life on earth from what I think is an uncommon perspective. A perspective that proposes all life is interconnected and interdependent. And that

each of us is a part of something much greater,
rather than just a life form moving randomly
through a finite life.

We Are Life

Arising out of these notes was the strong theme that the basic physical unit of all life on earth is the individual living single cell. Based on this insight, a definition of life would read as follows:

'Every living entity on earth consists of a single living cell, or multiples of single cells working together to their mutual advantage. Without the single cell no life would exist on earth. Each individual living cell is made up of a material body powered by life energy, which reproduces through a living cell and has the capacity to respond to and adapt to changes in its environment.'

Life Energy and the Life Force

Life energy is a natural energy that *powers* the life force. This natural energy, which exists throughout the universe, powers all life on earth *through* the life force. We cannot see or quantify the energy that enables dowsing, but with the right conditions we can see and utilise the effects of it. Similarly, we also cannot see or quantify the energy that enables life. However, we can see the manifestation of it in all living things. Both of these energies are natural elemental features of our universe.

The basic unit of all life on earth is the single living cell. To visualise how the life force powers each individual living cell, we can use the analogy of electrical energy and a light globe. When a light globe is lit, it is being powered by electricity, which is the product of electrical energy. We can see the resulting light radiating from the light globe. If the light globe fails, the electrical energy that provides electricity to the globe does not fail and will continue to power any other viable light globes in the circuit. The faulty light globe will not be able to draw on that power as it is damaged and will need to be discarded.

This same rationale can be applied to the life force generated by life energy. When a material body has life, it is being powered by the life force, which is the product of life energy. This energy manifests as the active biological processes inherent in all life forms. If an individual living cell is damaged to the extent that it can no longer act as a host for the life force, the life force is withdrawn from that cell. This individual cell will then die and be recycled. The life energy, however, does not die with it and continues to provide the life force to all other living cells on earth.

Several of the original notes referred to the life force as the soul. This is the part of us that is immortal because it has no physical form of its own and cannot be damaged or destroyed.

However, the life force is not omnipotent and has no control over events such as earthquakes, volcanoes, droughts or floods etc. as these are of the material world. Natural physical changes in the earth or its atmosphere do occur. For example, an earthquake in the earth's crust to relieve pressure, or variations in the weather because of changes in the environment and atmosphere. These are the natural outcomes of cause and effect.

The Material Body

For the life force to manifest as life on earth, it needs a suitable material body through which it can work to produce life. Just as electrical energy needs a physical light globe through which it can work to produce light. For all life on this planet, this suitable material body is the individual single cell.

A single living cell is basically a small bag of chemicals. When powered by the life force it becomes a living and biologically active single cell, able to reproduce by cell division. For the greater part of the time that life has been on earth, it has only been in the form of a single cell. The evolutionary advent of complex multicellular life enabled some single-cell life forms to work together to their mutual benefit. This enabled life to evolve increasingly sophisticated new multicellular life forms such as plants and animals.

Whether a cell exists as an individual single-celled life form, or has evolved as a specialised cell that is part of a complex multicellular life form, the life force itself still resides only in each single living cell. If a human suffers from the failure of a key bodily organ, most individual organs can now be transplanted from a suitable donor to replace the faulty organ. The individual cells that make up that organ will still retain their life force and continue to function, even though they have been transplanted into a different human body.

Conversely, when a replacement organ such as a heart is transplanted into a human whose heart had failed, the replacement heart continues to function. This enables all of the other individual cells in the recipient's body to also continue functioning and retain life.

Like all material things, the material body of each living cell will eventually fail and die. In death, the life force will withdraw, and the material body will be recycled back to the earth from which it came. The same process occurs when a multicellular life form such as a human fails and dies. However, as each individual cell is host to the life force, each cell will die individually when the multicellular life form is unable to provide a functioning body. Death occurs as each cell's life-support systems progressively shut down.

Each living material body is able to reproduce through a living cell. In doing so, the ability to host the life force is passed on in a similar way that a hand on the shoulder can pass on the ability to dowse.

The process of passing on the life force from one generation to the next is primarily through cell division, which has essentially been the same process since life first appeared on our planet. The original life force that powered the first life on earth is still the same life force that powers all life today.

One noticeable point is that the definition of life at the beginning of this chapter allows for a virus to be classified as a parasitic life form, whereas contemporary science does not normally define a virus as alive.

Where Did Life Come From?

Aeons ago, in the infinity of space, a vast cloud of dust, gas and other debris collapsed inwards onto itself. Over time these materials coalesced to become our solar system. The materials that became the building blocks of our sun and its planets were already very old, having been recycled as star systems many times before. Scattered throughout the debris of these earlier star systems were what one of the notes described as the spores of life.

Each of these individual spores already contained life in the form of the minute germ of a material body. This already hosted the life force, as it had been in contact with the life force at some time in the distant past. Being so small and basic, these spores of life were able to survive for untold ages in the extreme conditions of outer space and suspended animation.

Many spores of life would have perished in the turmoil of our solar system's formation. However, as the sun and planets began to coalesce from the cloud of dust, gas and debris, environments that were conducive to life gradually became available. Many of the surviving spores of life settled into these habitable new environments. Wherever a spore found a suitable environment, it slowly became activated, developing and adapting into its new surroundings.

To do this, the spore, powered by the life force with which it was already endowed, developed and grew its material form from the germ of the material body. It did this by using the materials and conditions available to it in its immediate environment. These spores are the foundation of all life on earth.

Ever since planetary life was established, it has continued to evolve and adapt. This has allowed it to become more complex and better suited to the earth's various environments as they changed and evolved over time. As individual spores encountered varying materials and conditions, each of these individual spores developed unique strategies and abilities. These enabled them to not only survive, but to become more adaptable and robust in a changing environment. Each of the spores that successfully adapted to their particular environment developed into single-celled life forms. These life forms were then able to procreate by simple cell division.

Life arose from these spores many times on the ancient earth. Just as each of these spores of life had a common ancestor, all life on earth has a common ancestor. Thus, life on earth is much older than the earth itself. The spores of life would also have been distributed widely throughout our early solar system. Each contained life energy that enabled it to develop and grow in suitable environments.

Any of the spores of life that adapted to environments elsewhere in our solar system would have encountered different conditions, materials and atmospheres to that on earth. So even though we have a common ancestor, this life would most likely be very alien to us.

As mentioned previously, initially all life on this planet consisted solely of single-cell life forms. Each of the spores of life that developed as a living cell would have done so in an environment that was unique. Unique in the mix of minerals, chemicals, moisture levels, temperature etc., which cradled its development.

The early earth itself was much more geologically active then than it is now. There was virtually no oxygen in the earth's early atmosphere, and the sun itself radiated much less heat than it does now. Therefore, life on the early earth developed to survive in the conditions at that time. However, as the conditions changed, life evolved and changed to suit the changing environment. It has continued to evolve ever since as the conditions for life continually change.

The short life cycles of single-cell life forms allowed for enormous numbers of generations in countless unique environments. Given the vast amount of time over which single-cell life forms were able to adapt and evolve, there have been single-cell life forms for virtually every set of environmental conditions on the planet.

These single-cell life forms were the foundations of the vast array of life on earth today. Occasionally, variations arose in some of these life forms. Any variation that better suited the environment soon became dominant. With conditions continually changing, evolution of life was on its way.

Life itself will prove to be relatively common throughout the universe. Much less common and perhaps even unique to life on earth has been the evolution of multicellular life. This has led to the rise of conscious, intelligent life forms with all the abilities and potential this brings for us.

Why Are We Here?

The life force powered by the life energy is our starting point. It is the one constant of all life on earth. It has been present to power every earthly life form that has ever existed. The basic role of earth life is to harvest energy from the material world, but the ultimate role and potential of life is currently beyond our comprehension.

The purpose of evolution is not just the adaptation of an individual species to an environment. It is the adaptation and evolution of each environment so that the environment itself is balanced and sustainable. Ultimately, the various environments on earth will also be in balance and sustainable in relation to each other, planet wide.

As the worldwide environment becomes more stable and balanced, the more evolution on earth will be focused on the ongoing *nurture* and *development* of all life – instead of continually adjusting life to bring the planet's environments into balance. When life on earth reaches this point it will be able to reach its full potential.

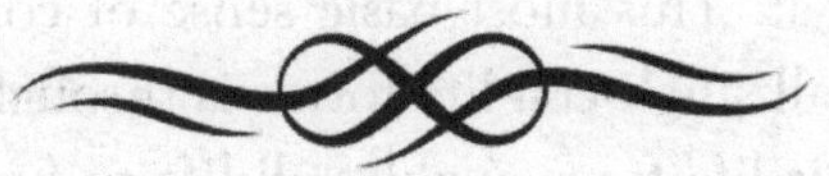

Mother Nature

The concept that all earthly life is just the one living multicellular entity was one of the last major concepts to reveal itself in the notes. Once it did, it quickly took its place as a key part in this earth-life story. As I first became aware of this new concept, I started thinking of it as the network of life. However, when writing this chapter, I found that almost all of the old notes that touched on this subject referred to it as Mother Nature, so Mother Nature it became.

All life on this planet is interconnected at a cellular level through the life force. This connectedness between all living single cells is not something that we can be aware of consciously. This sense of connectedness and the part of our brain that processes it are from a time before consciousness as we know it existed here. Even today, the majority of single-cell life is not conscious as we know it. This most basic sense of connection between all single-cell life forms is through the life force. This life force enables all life to function as one planet-wide multicellular organism, which the notes refer to as Mother Nature.

If we as individual human beings consider ourselves as a functioning multicellular organism, then we can use this as the model for Mother Nature. She is the ultimate multicellular organism.

The human body is made up of trillions of individual living cells, all interconnected and communicating with each other through the life force, enabling the human body to function as an individual life form. This network of interconnected living cells manages and controls every function and organ of the human body, including the brain, without any control or awareness from the conscious mind. In doing so, the human body is able to operate as a single multicellular life form.

Mother Nature is the highest level of multicellular life and is made up of all life on earth, functioning as a single entity. She is made up of trillions of individual life forms, ranging from single cell microbes to the most complex multicellular organisms such as humans, all inter-connected with each other via life energy.

This is a planet-wide version of the same process that evolved into the human body, but on a much more extensive scale. Mother Nature is all life working together as a world-encompassing multicellular life form.

The complex human body developed a conscious sense of self to manage and control the continued survival and progress of that human body. Mother Nature also developed appropriate senses to manage and control the continued survival and progress of her network of life on earth.

The evolving human mind has individual consciousness, which allows the use of conscious thought and free will. This enables us to plan and guide the actions of that human body in its best interests.

Again, using the human example as a model is helpful when visualising an older and much larger multicellular life form that has also developed a form of consciousness. This planet-wide consciousness can intercede, plan and guide the function and development of life in *its* best interests. One way to help us visualise a planet-wide Mother Nature is to reword the old adage, 'We can't see the forest for the trees,' to 'We can't see Mother Nature for the individual life forms around us.'

In nature, each level of life is ultimately dependent on the levels around it to function. Any significant change that damages or alters any part of the natural world has the potential to alter the balance and stability of Mother Nature itself. Mother Nature connects all levels of life so that together they function as one world-encompassing organism, without any control or awareness of the individual life forms themselves.

Over a vast period of time, life evolved an immense variety of single-cell life forms. These enabled an almost infinite and diverse range of capabilities. The mutually beneficial cooperation and combination of these very different types of cells were the advent of multicellular life on earth.

While there are now enormous numbers of different multicellular life forms such as humans, horses, oak trees and ostriches, there are only a relatively small number of group patterns. All mammals, for example, have basically the same body plan yet have evolved as a blue whale, a horse, a human or a mouse, each to suit their environment.

Yet evolution has produced each of these from the same first mammal, which itself evolved from even earlier life forms. Evolution has a toolkit of genes and switches that it can use to modify any one of these mammals, and all other life forms for that matter, to better suit a new environment. The primary requirement is time.

Every living cell contains the basic genetic information of its direct ancestors back to the beginning of life on earth. The functions and abilities of these ancestors are still latent in each living cell.

The vast array of specialised cells that life has developed is the toolkit for evolution on earth. Physical life forms are continually being adapted and created to best adapt life to its environment.

The evolution of complex multicellular life takes time as evolutionary change takes place at the single-cell level and gradually works up the chain. Single-cell life forms are able to evolve very quickly. It is only the single cell that needs to adapt and the life cycle of each generation is short. A good example would be how single-cell bacteria are able to adapt very quickly to antibiotics, yet it would take a good deal longer for a mouse to evolve into something like a blue whale.

Life is continually evolving and adapting to changes in the earth's living environments. There are life forms currently living in the deepest parts of the ocean, under the ice in Antarctica, around deep-sea thermal vents and deep below the earth's surface.

Some of these life forms can survive on little or no oxygen, in extremes of temperature where we could not survive, and have life processes very different to ours. However, they are still related to us, and their unique abilities may be critical in the future by allowing life to adapt and survive major changes in our environment.

We humans need to be more aware of the multiple levels of life that we are dependent on for our very survival. Single-cell microbes are by far the most populous life on earth, and are also the foundation of Mother Nature. Microbes are of critical importance in the soil and the oceans. They are necessary for the plants, which use photosynthesis to grow, and on which all the higher levels of life are dependent. The microbes within the bodies of the higher levels of life, including humans, are also critical for the functioning and survival of these higher-level life forms. We stand on their shoulders.

Mother Nature is continually striving to develop a balanced and sustainable mix of life forms to continue her upward evolution. She does not specifically need humans; she needs the most suitable selection of life forms. These then become the stable and sustainable foundation of life. This foundation allows Mother Nature to continually evolve and develop more complex and increasingly capable life forms, whatever they may be.

Consciousness and Self

There were not a lot of notes that referred directly to consciousness and self. Those that did described the conscious sense of self as the single most important difference between humans and other earth life. One note was particularly wide-ranging and I think worthy of including verbatim as follows:

'Who are we? The colony that makes up each of us is a complex assemblage of living cells. Each has evolved to perform a specific function, and in combination as a colony allows our body to function as an individual entity. Much of the day-to-day functioning of our body, such as breathing, heartbeat, digestion etc. is controlled by our subconscious mind. However, in many highly evolved entities (including humans) the mind also has an evolved consciousness, which is effectively a super sense. This allows the entity to think and react to perceived threats or opportunities using the combined inputs of older senses such as touch, sight, sound etc. It also uses the memory of previous experiences as part of the conscious sense of self.'

Other aspects of consciousness, particularly in humans, are the ability to visualise based on experience and memory. We use this ability to plan ahead for circumstances that potentially may happen. We will also become more aware of and able to recognise new concepts and possibilities that open up to us.

Consciousness itself was a major step forward in the independence and capability of multicellular life. The sense of self that arises out of consciousness gives humans significant ability to affect Mother Nature and the future direction of planetary life.

The precursor to conscious life was in the form of rudimentary abilities. These abilities enabled primitive life forms to sense any changes, such as variations in chemicals, temperature or light, in their environment. As conscious life evolved, new senses, and the effective use of these new senses, continued to be refined and developed. This greatly enhanced the survival of the life forms that possessed these abilities.

From its inception and even in its most basic form, consciousness has been a key factor in developing multicellular life. It is one of the evolutionary drivers of 'survival of the fittest'.

The various simple nervous systems that had enabled the basic consciousness of earlier life continued to interact and evolve in the higher life forms. These eventually merged to become the brain. A key function of the newly evolved brain was to centralise the input from the five conscious senses of sight, touch, smell, taste and hearing to become the centre of awareness and eventually the seat of consciousness.

In addition to the five senses mentioned above there is also a sixth sense. This sense uses the connection of life energy between all living cells as its channel of communication. The sixth sense is from a very early period in the evolution of life. As such, it works through a part of our brain and nervous system that predates the rise of consciousness. As consciousness became a key driver in the growing success and development of the higher life forms, conscious thought dominated. It mostly drowned out the older sixth sense, to the extent that this older capability rarely impinges on our conscious selves.

I personally found the notes about the sixth sense very interesting as I had an experience at about the age of twenty that fits in with the way the sixth sense seems to work. I was working in a regional area at the time. Two friends and I had discovered trotting racing. Race meetings were held each Saturday night at one of several country towns, on a rotating basis. I had a car that was almost as old as I was, but it was still able to exceed the speed limit quite comfortably, if not safely. On this particular evening, the trotting race meeting was in a country town about an hours' drive away via a two-lane country road. The drive up was uneventful but fast. After the meeting, we set out on the return journey in the same manner.

It was a dark night. There was virtually no other traffic on the road, and the old car was humming along as fast as it could go. About half-way back I suddenly noticed that I'd subconsciously slowed down considerably, so I got up to speed again. But I now felt very uneasy driving that fast. Slowing down again but consciously this time, I tried to look around but there was no light in sight anywhere in the blackness. Being an old car, the headlights did not shine very far ahead, so I kept travelling at the much slower speed – all the time wondering why.

Coming over the crest of a hill, I slowed down even more. In the blackness I noticed a small light ahead. It was to one side and moving towards the road we were on. As I continued driving, the headlights started to illuminate freight train carriages that were moving slowly across the road just ahead of us. At about the same time, the train guard came running along the train line and onto the road waving his light.

At the initial speed I had been driving, I would not have been able to stop in time, and the shock of that realisation is still etched clearly in my memory. At the time, I had no idea why I subconsciously had slowed down. The concept of the sixth sense is the best answer I have been able to find to date. At the time I first slowed down, I had no sense of danger. The initial slowing down was not done consciously, but whatever it was, it was strong enough for me to continue driving slowly until I could work out what was going on.

Our Sense of Self

Another function of the newly evolved brain is as the control centre for consciousness. As our sense of self is an outcome of consciousness, our brain is also the centre of our sense of self. Self-awareness and the ability for abstract thought are both relatively recent advances in the evolution of consciousness. Humans are the major beneficiaries of both of these advances.

The development and growth of language was the trigger enabling rapid advances in both self-awareness and abstract thought. These advances led to major changes in the balance of life on earth, notably the rapid rise of humans as the dominant species on earth.

Language allowed the large-scale accumulation and transfer of knowledge between individuals. It also became a framework to hold and develop abstract ideas in the mind. These newly acquired abilities allowed humans to use imagination, visualisation and the communication of ideas, turning abstract thoughts and concepts into reality. These enhanced abilities also allowed the world of possibilities to broaden. They opened the human mind to new concepts such as empathy and compassion. They facilitated the awareness of spirituality and religion. These abilities also supported new ways of expression through art and storytelling.

As the use of language expanded, virtually limitless possibilities opened up for our species. This kick-started the evolutionary process of developing new neural pathways in the human brain. In turn, this permitted humans to make more effective use of their new capabilities.

An increase in the use of abstract thought and imagination triggered evolution to work as a feedback loop – each time there was better use of our brain function, there was correlating physical improvement in our brain and how it functioned. The result was an ongoing cycle of evolutionary improvement in our conscious abilities, whereupon improved brain function prompted better use of our brain, leading to more improvements in brain function etc.

This cycle of continued improvement in both the capabilities of the human brain and our ability to find new ways to use it, continues to the present day. Humans now develop and adapt to a continuous flow of new technologies, all enabled by our use of language.

Conscious thought and individual free will are abilities that give humans a much greater range of options, such as allowing an individual to make decisions based on conscious thought rather than instinctive reaction. This ability to analyse and then make a calculated decision gives us new ways of dealing with the challenges that may confront us. As environments change, conscious decisions may give us an answer to a threat that we have not encountered before, where an instinctive reaction may not be the best response.

Humans are not born with a ready-made sense of self, and this awareness develops as a learned experience via our conscious mind. We have evolved to be totally dependent on our family group at birth and during early childhood.

We have a very long period of childhood, which allows us to grow and develop as part of the environment we are born into. This enables us to develop a sense of self that is tuned for survival in that particular environment.

What each human thinks of as self is actually our consciousness creating a sense of awareness of self, and this is what we feel and understand to be ourselves. While our body is a living entity because of the living cells that together make up our body, our awareness of self is not a living entity. It is an understanding and identity that is powered by our consciousness.

Life energy and the conscious mind with its sense of self are both fundamental aspects of human life, but these are not consciously connected. However, our thoughts and experiences, particularly those that involve emotion, are subconsciously transferred between our conscious mind and the life energy via the life force.

Anything that is transferred through to the life energy becomes part of the experience of that life energy. Even when our physical body dies, along with our physical awareness of self, our lifetime of emotions and experiences will always be an integral part of the universal life energy, of which we are all a part.

Human conscious thought and capability has evolved to the point where we are often able to alter our environment to suit us, rather than us evolving to suit the environment that we were born into. Our success in doing this and our subsequent plague-like population growth is creating a rapidly growing imbalance of life on earth.

One of the old notes warns specifically that if we are not able to find a sustainable balance, then Mother Nature will. However, consciousness has also given humans the knowledge, resources and capabilities to guide and shape the future of planetary life for the long-term benefit of life, rather than the more primitive 'survival of the fittest'. Our future is in our hands.

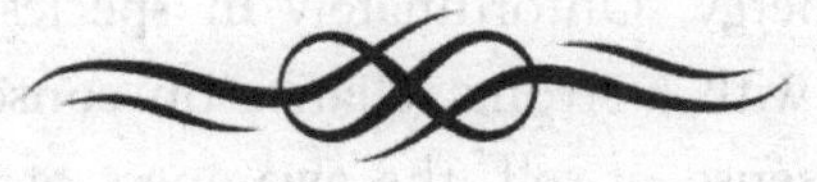

Spirituality and Religion

There are quite a few of the old notes that contribute to this chapter. Mostly as an alternative way of understanding life as part of the natural world, and also how we, as spiritual beings, are a part of it. In the chapter, 'We are Life', the life force is also referred to as the soul. The soul is comparable to concepts and beliefs found in most religions, both past and present. There is also one note, which begins with, 'God is all life; all life is God'. This infers that while the life force is often referred to as the soul, the life energy that powers the life force is the energy often referred to as God

Spirituality is not the same thing as religion. They are related in that religion is an outcome of spirituality, but spirituality does not need religion to exist. Spirituality is our physical mind being subconsciously aware of its continuous connection to life energy. All life is born with this connection to life energy. Unfortunately in species such as humans, with a strong reliance on consciousness and our sense of self, the awareness of this connection is mostly drowned out by the conscious mind.

Religions on the other hand are created through the mind and hand of man. Mankind has a long history of religious awareness. The advent of language enabled the earliest communal thinking and creation of stories to help explain the 'sixth-sense' presence of something greater than our conscious self.

Over the ages since then, the various human groupings have attempted to explain this sense of a nonmaterial presence through the eyes of the contemporary culture of the day, using the knowledge and understanding of the time. These insights and stories handed down from our ancestors are the foundation of communal spiritual belief, and of the religions that have been built on their foundations.

As humans are not born with a ready-made sense of self, evolution has programmed each newborn human child to come into the world with minimal instinctive survival skills, and they are totally dependent on adults at the time of birth. This evolutionary trait is an advanced survival advantage as it allows each new human child to adapt to and function in the environment that it was born into. This adaptation is necessary because human societies are very complex.

Around the world, the human environments into which a child may be born all differ in their cultures, practices, language and beliefs. The threats and dangers to a young child, and the life skills that they may need, would also be very different in each of these human environments. The care and support of the parents and the wider community allows the newborn child to be guided, grow into and become a part of its particular complex human community. The more that the child's conscious mind is conditioned to be part of its environment, the more its awareness of its subconscious connection to the life force is either nourished or diminished.

From birth, the child is immersed within its society. As it develops and grows, it quickly becomes attuned to and part of the immediate world around it. After a couple of years, the child's mind will have developed and experienced enough to develop its own basic sense of self. Over the following years, the child firms up their understanding of who they are. This sense of self is highly dependent on the culture they were born into, which includes language as well as religious and spiritual beliefs.

The longer a person builds their foundation of beliefs and understanding of the world, based on their learned culture and experience, the harder it is for them to accept and assimilate any new information that does not fit into their beliefs.

In cases where new information is particularly compelling, it may require the dismantling of part of that initial foundation to accept the new understanding. This is not an easy thing to do when the foundation has been long established, and particularly if their foundation of beliefs had worked well in the past.

Life in all of its forms needs to harvest energy to sustain itself. Once those basic needs are met, life has the potential to continue evolving to a level that we cannot yet comprehend. Life has come a long way since the first spores of life arrived on the planet, and Mother Nature will continue to evolve life towards that potential.

We are life, and as humans, we are the most evolved form of earth life at the present time. We are the best placed to be at the forefront of this ongoing evolution. The continuous feedback loop described in the chapter 'Consciousness and Self' started with the advent of language, and it continues to this day.

Language is the great upward driver of evolution. However, the continuous improvement in our conscious and technical capacities has reached a level where we need to refocus and work together as a species.

We are at a point where survival of the fittest and self-benefit has served us well. But with our technical dominance of life, we must change our focus as a species to the survival and benefit of Mother Nature. Otherwise, we could well become a handicap to sustainable earth life. For Mother Nature, any endeavours should be beneficial and not detrimental to life. With that as the primary understanding of our species, we would have the potential to be a significant, long-term benefit to this planet.

Over recent generations, humans have virtually swamped the earth with their huge population increases. We are decimating other life forms and environments in a bid to feed and maintain this ever-growing human population.

We have been able to do this because we can, and with our technology we have the ability to manage every life form on the planet. To the other life forms on earth, humans as a species have the power of the gods over their life and death.

All of the major religions are from a time when humans were a part of life, rather than the omnipotent beings that their technology now enables.

These religions have focused almost solely on human wellbeing and benefit rather than on life itself. We have come to a point where religious and spiritual beliefs need to be updated to reflect the world we now live in. We, as a species, now need to have a united focus on Mother Nature's wellbeing and benefit. She is the network of all life, which we are a part of and totally dependent on. With a focus on ourselves as a part of life, rather than on us as an individual, we should be able to feel comfortable with our beliefs and goals without the need to believe that another person's beliefs and goals are wrong.

Our systems of government are similarly from past eras. With our uncontrolled population growth and unsustainable use of resources, we urgently need to modify our hierarchy of government to create and manage a planet-wide environment. This environment needs to support the survival of all life, not just 'survival of the strongest'.

Mother Nature strives to maintain the best mix of life on earth. This allows the continued and sustainable evolution and development of more complex life forms. Humans as the currently dominant life forms need to support and enable Mother Nature in its stewardship role. If we are unable to use our technology to return the network of life to a sustainable balance, then Mother

Nature will do it for us. We need to be aware that we are a part of Mother Nature. What we as individuals do to our world, we are doing to ourselves, to our children and our children's children.

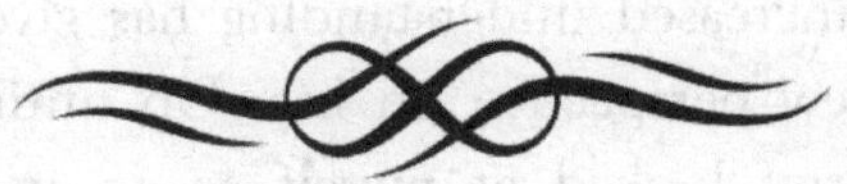

The More I think About It, The Bigger It Gets

Since I started on this project of converting the treasure trove of old notes into a book, my awareness of what life is has grown as the story has developed. Each time I write or rewrite a chapter, I feel that I am moving a little closer to a basic understanding of the overview of life that the notes seem to contain. At the same time, I am also becoming more aware of just how vast, complex and integrated life on earth is, and that we humans are such a tiny part of it.

With this growing awareness, it is becoming increasingly important to me to present what I think is a unique understanding of life, in the best way that I can. The more I understand the story that is rising up out of the old notes, the more I believe that this story is coming through me and is not of me.

This increased understanding has given me a totally new perspective on life. Up until now, I have always looked at myself as an individual, striving to live life in a positive and satisfying way in the eyes of my family, my community and myself. The benchmarks that I have been using to measure my success have been the values of my peer group and my childhood conditioning. However, as I work with and gain a better understanding of the old jotted notes, I am moving more and more towards the Mother Nature concept. Where life on earth is a single planet-wide organism, and that we are part of something much greater than ourselves as individuals.

I quote the following paragraph verbatim as it describes the difficulty that I am currently experiencing in transposing this new awareness to paper:

'Language was an incredible advance in human development and communication, but it is also restrictive in that each word has a defined meaning. Whereas thoughts often have a greater breadth and shades of meaning that words do not adequately express. Language has allowed us to structure and express our ideas, but it also tends to mould and pare down an idea into a black-and-white concept that can be expressed in words. It can't then pass on the full visualisation, intuition and concept of the idea. This limitation of language is particularly relevant in religion as it gives rise to the many different ways of seeing the same thing, and each is as valid as the other.'

Even though we as humans have rapidly increased our ability to dominate and change our environment through innovation and technology, we have lost sight of the fact that we are part of Mother Nature. Our recent blind destruction of the living environment worldwide is having the same catastrophic effect on life as major geological catastrophes have had in the past. With our newly acquired power to change our world, we need to also quickly acquire the understanding that we are an interdependent part of the earth's living environment. We need to regain and act on that knowledge very quickly, as the longer we continue to foul our own nest, the more catastrophic will be the resultant consequences.

One conscious habit that has stood us in good stead in the past may become our Achilles heel as we continue into the future. This habit is our propensity to accept perception as reality. Our consciousness can be programmed by personal or external experiences and influences, and the results of that programming are regarded as reality by that particular consciousness.

The complexities and technologies of the modern world are increasingly enabling other parties to manipulate and condition our personal perception to their advantage. This has been happening for thousands of years but is now happening on such a massive scale and on so many levels that it will redefine our future.

We have mass education systems today. We also co-exist with the massive reach of big technology and media entities, disseminating their information. Humans are being squeezed through a narrower and narrower system of education and thought. This churns out millions and millions of people with similar thoughts, expectations and perceptions. The conditioning of our perception is now a massive industry with countless beneficiaries, the largest and most established of these being religion, politics and big business in all their forms.

We each need to be responsible for ourselves as we each have the knowledge of what is right or wrong deep within us. The more we exercise that knowledge, the stronger we become as an individual. We should also keep in mind the fact that anyone that stands to benefit in some way from the advice they offer is not an infallible source of advice.

Another potential consequence for humans as we rush towards our future is that we are still evolving. We are already less robust physically, have smaller teeth and are more fragile than our ancestors. This may be offset against the fact that we have also come a long way with the use of our mind in improving our imagination, visualisation and communication.

The human brain is very adaptable. Just like our muscles, which strengthen and develop to match their use in our environment, our brain adapts to the stimulations of our environment, particularly in our formative years. If we are born into a situation where walking long distances is the norm, then our muscles and bodies are optimised to that requirement. If we are sedentary and look at screens all day and allow technology to do a lot of our thinking, our bodies and brains will be optimised as best as they can to that environment.

Over recent generations, we have become increasingly reliant on technology and in particular artificial intelligence. The more we develop and depend on assistance devices and technology of every type, the more evolution will gradually reallocate the physical resources and brain function that previously enabled these functions.

Brainpower is a very energy-hungry function and is demand driven, and when the demand decreases, so will the bodily resources allocated to it. Even now there are changes in the neural pathways of our newer generations as they become more and more interfaced and reliant on technology. If we don't use it, we lose it.

The human lifetime is too short to notice the huge changes that we as a species have initiated in our world over the last few thousand years. We need to see and visualise an overview of life and evolution over longer periods of time to put things into perspective. Our minds cannot comprehend the enormous amount of time it has already taken for the evolution of life to reach the stage where humans even became possible.

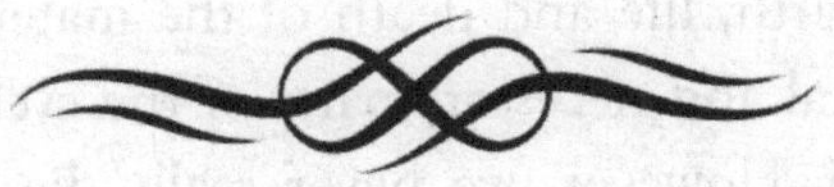

Death and Dying

The material body is of the earth. The evolution of earth life is the process of countless generations of life forms each reproducing a slightly more evolved material version of itself. At death, each material body is recycled back to the earth. Even though the material body returns to the earth, the life energy that animated it carries the knowledge and experience of that material body forward. This then becomes part of the knowledge and experience of life, which is eternal.

Every material body will eventually fail as all material things do. With the withdrawal of the life force and the material body recycled, a generation of life has completed its cycle and made room for the next. This is all part of the ongoing evolution of life. It is an unending process that develops and supports the ever-more complex and highly evolved life forms.

The birth, life and death of the material body are natural and necessary parts of the cycle of material life. However, we never really die as all of the experiences, emotions and memories of every physical body become part of the eternal life energy through the life force as they occur. Many past and present religions were aware of the life force as that part of us that carries on after death, and refer to it as the soul. Our material body will die, but our soul, which is the life force, powered by life energy, is immortal.

The process of birth, life and death takes place at the cellular level, but with the evolution of multicellular life forms, the process becomes a little more complex. Colonies of individual cells are now able to work together in the form of self-contained life forms, and at this time, the most evolved and complex of these multicellular life forms are humans.

When a human body is unable to continue its function as a host to the life energy, the entire complex of living cells, which together make up that human body, will each gradually die. The human body can only function and continue to host the life force when all the key organs of the body are able to function.

As each individual cell in the body is host to the life energy, each cell of each organ will die individually as the body's life support system fails and the major organs shut down. When the brain cells, which support our consciousness and our sense of self, have died then our material self has died. While writing this book, I have come to understand that as long as our major organs are still alive and functioning, our hearing and brain are also still functioning, even when we are not conscious.

It was a relief for me when I first learned of the above. For many years I had felt that I'd not been able to say goodbye to my father before he passed away. When my father was diagnosed with terminal cancer in his fifties, I was settled and working at the other end of the country. As there was nothing that the doctors could do for him, he was allowed to go home where my mother nursed him and kept me updated on his condition.

There was no such thing as cell phones at that time. As my father was confined to his bed, we were not able to talk over the phone, but it was all organised for me to go home to see him in the upcoming holidays. A few weeks before the holidays I received an urgent telegram saying that my father had taken a sudden turn for the worse and that I needed to come home quickly. I caught a plane and arrived home the following afternoon, but by that time dad was in a coma and there was no way to communicate with him.

The next morning I was sitting beside his bed holding his hand, and he seemed to be in a deep sleep taking long, slow breaths. Even though he was not awake, I leaned over and told him how much I loved him and gave him a kiss on the forehead, then sat down again while still holding his hand. About ten minutes later my father passed away. It has been of great comfort to me to know that my father would have been able to hear me, and know that I was there before he died. Maybe he had even been waiting and holding on until I was able to get there.

While our material bodies run their course and are replaced by the next material life cycle, our life experiences remain as part of the life energy. As we are all part of life energy through the life force, we are always connected to and are a part of all those who have gone before us, and who will come after us.

'Love doesn't end with dying or leave with the last breath.
For someone you've loved deeply, love doesn't end with death.'

John Addey (1920 – 1982)

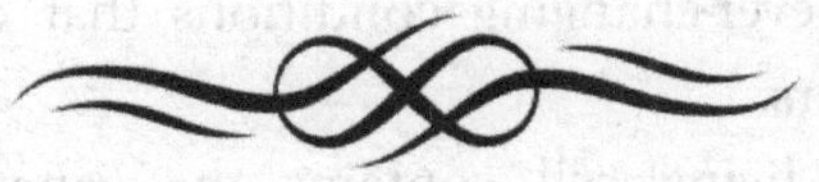

Does Mother Nature Have An Agenda?

We multicellular humans have evolved our consciousness and our sense of self. So too has Mother Nature, the oldest and largest multicellular life form on our planet. She has also evolved the appropriate senses to manage and guide the continued development of all life on the planet.

The evolution of life is not just the change and adaptation of an individual species to suit an environment. It is the change and development of all the different species in all the different environments towards a single interconnected and balanced network.

Over time, Mother Nature has developed a vast array of specialised cells to meet the changes and setbacks to life as they arise. These cells are part of the evolutionary toolkit from which new or revised physical life forms are adapted or created to suit the ever-changing conditions that earth life encounters.

Every living cell contains the genetic information of its ancestors right back to its original ancestor on earth. The more complex and varied the evolutionary path of a cell, the greater the variety and number of traits, both active and latent, that exist in their genes.

Mother Nature employs many different strategies in the ongoing evolution of life. For example, species such as animals (including humans), reptiles, birds, fish etc. are driven by self-interest. However, bees and ants exist as societies where each individual has the interest and preservation of the group as its motivation. In essence, these complex societies are yet another form of multicellular life. Plants do not have consciousness as we know it but are able to respond to changes in their environment. All of the above alternatives have been developed by Mother Nature to occupy the various niches in life.

There are also alternative strategies available should the environment change so much that one of these strategies should become the most viable. These strategies mostly coexist and interact with other variations to create a sustainable environment. They use survival of the fittest to choose the life forms that are the best suited. Life itself is also a factor in this ongoing competition for survival as it continually alters the chemistry of its environment just through the process of living.

When an environment is basically in balance, there is often little noticeable change. What is actually happening is a steady and continuous fine-tuning of each life form in the environment to improve its adaption to that place. Every now and then, one of these small changes will suddenly prove to be a significant advantage to its recipient, and this will set off an urgent flurry of change and evolution to return that environment to balance.

Some species do experience a significant advantage and is overly successful to the extent that it causes rapid change to the balance of life. When this happens, factors such as disease, starvation and aggressive competition for resources have historically been instrumental in bringing an environment quickly back into balance.

Our earth is currently under rapidly increasing stress with the human population growing at an exponential rate, and it is already at what seems to be an unsustainable level. We humans are managing to stay ahead of the curve for the short term, with innovation and medical advances, but ultimately the pressure to bring the environment back into a sustainable state of balance will force change.

The greatest rate of evolution takes place after mass extinctions. Significant gaps often occur after these major events where there are no suitable survivor species available to fill these gaps. However, over longer periods of time, evolution will adapt other life forms to suit these vacant niches. Every capability of our direct ancestors still exists in our genes, and the key to how a species will evolve depends on switching on or off the various combinations of triggers in each of our genes.

Most triggers are predisposed to switch on in line with our most recent ancestors, but over time and under changing conditions, the switch combinations can change to better suit the current conditions.

The more I read and understand the story of life contained in these notes, the more I am convinced that Mother Nature is working to a flexible but consistent agenda. There is little in the notes to suggest what the end result of this agenda might be, but what they do show is that this agenda has been in process since life first arrived on earth.

As I look back over the history of life on this planet, it indicates that the first stage of life's agenda was to establish a robust foundation to harvest the abundant energy available, including energy from the sun. This foundation consisted of the evolution and build-up of an enormous range of diverse single-cell life forms. These were insurance that there would always be suitable life forms able to survive, regardless of how much an environment may have changed.

When the aims of the first stage were achieved, the second stage was initiated. The second stage aided multicellular life in all its forms. Survival of the fittest has been the main driver of the ongoing evolution of these rapidly evolving multicellular life forms. This allowed the most successful combinations of abilities and skills to be tested and developed over millions of generations. The species that evolved to be the most resilient and adaptable to date has recently emerged as the dominant species on the planet. This species has proved to be humans.

We are now several thousand years into the third stage. This stage seems to be where life continually strives to evolve to higher levels of consciousness and ever more complex and capable higher life forms. However, there are no indications in any of the notes as to what this steady upward evolution is aimed at, or why.

The long history of the increasing resilience, complexity and abilities of the higher life forms would indicate that the current evolutionary direction is towards something beyond our current abilities. At this stage we cannot see or envisage what the ultimate goal is. This may still be for survival of the fittest to decide.

Can Humans Be Part Of The Future?

Humans made a very late appearance in the history of life on earth. Even when our primate ancestors did make an appearance, it was still a struggle for them to hold their place in a very competitive world. It was only with the advent of language, which triggered the rapid increase in our abilities, that humans gained a significant competitive edge. This advantage enabled humans to quickly become earth's dominant life form.

The newfound adaptability and innovation of modern humans gave them the abilities and skills to survive and thrive through major climate change, including the ice age. They were also able to make significant changes in the way they interacted with their environment with the innovation of farming and the rapid increase in their development and use of new technology. As a species, we are currently the dominant life form; however, as a species, this position is ours to lose if we are unable to grow into the responsibilities of this role.

The very traits that allowed us to dominate other life forms may also be our downfall. We need to become more aware of the fact that we are ultimately dependent on Mother Nature. She is the interconnected and interdependent network of all life through which we have evolved and are still very much a part of.

In the earlier chapter on Mother Nature, the analogy of a complex human body was used as an example of how a single multicellular life form could function planet-wide. We can also use that same analogy to illustrate how a human body cell goes rogue and begins to multiply itself to its own ends.

We refer to this as cancer, and if it is not controlled or excised, it will eventually destroy the human body that is its host. We humans have reached a point where as a species, we are capable of, and are currently making, significant changes to the earth's living environments.

Unfortunately, our newfound dominance can be likened to a cancer as it has self-interest and greed as its major drivers. This is substantially degrading rather than nurturing and enhancing the role of Mother Nature. With our unsustainable population growth and subsequent overuse of the world's resources, we are blindly dismantling and destroying our own living environment.

The significant advantage that we humans have over other life forms is that our evolved conscious abilities have allowed us to be spectacularly successful as a species in a world of survival of the fittest. However, these same conscious abilities have also given us the ability to comprehend what we are doing. We therefore have the capability to move away from the survival of the fittest mindset to a mindset where we can be an integral part of the future.

Working parallel with and as part of Mother Nature to create a sustainable future will require us all to make major changes in our mindset. Thankfully, we humans are intelligent and adaptable enough when the pressure to do so becomes sufficient. However, the longer we do nothing, the greater the disruptions will be when this pressure does become sufficient to force change.

The sheer scale of the change that we need to make to be part of a sustainable future will require consensus and unity. We can only make the necessary shifts when humans in general have common goals and expectations.

The time for capitalism, patriotism, racism, borders and self-interest is passing. We need to find a worldwide integrated system of government, which takes our human traits into account, but still works. We humans have evolved as part of the natural world and are totally dependent on the natural world for our wellbeing. By changing our living environment to suit our own ends instead of adapting to and working with it (and all other life forms that also depend on it), we isolate ourselves from the very systems that sustain us.

With our evolved capabilities, we have the opportunity and the ability to play a significant role in shaping earth's future progress and development – to the benefit of all life that coexists with us. Fundamentally, all life on earth is of the one life energy, and together we make up environments where we are interconnected and interdependent on each other.

With this book moving towards its conclusion, I have been reflecting on how my understanding of life has changed from the mindset of a self-contained individual to one where I am part of something much greater.

When I began writing this story, I made the comment that this was a good way to utilise the old notes I had collected over so many years. But what I have found during the writing process is that this has been one of the most satisfying, empowering and life-changing things I have ever done. It has significantly changed my understanding of life on earth and our place in it, and has also opened my eyes to the huge problems and disruption that we are creating – not only for ourselves but for Mother Nature as well. This, in itself, opens the gates to a new and far more important story: understanding how we can be part of the future solution rather than part of the problem.

Afterword

As I prepare *We are Life* for publication, it is obvious to me that this is not the full story. *We are Life* tells us who we are and where we are now. However, the story of how we can be part of the future of life on earth has still to unfold. There are many of the old notes that were not used as they did not fit into the subject matter of *We are Life*. My goal is to utilise these notes in another volume. This second volume will light a way, empowering humans to be a solution rather than a problem for all future life on this planet.

ABOUT THE AUTHOR

Author Peter Griffiths has condensed seventy-five
years of life experience and observation into his
debut book *We Are Life*. With uncanny insight and
refreshing candour, he provides theories on some of
life's fundamental questions, such as 'What is life?'
and 'Why are we here?' He also masterfully points
out that life on earth is currently at a crossroads, and
we humans have a big part to play in which direction
it takes.

Peter has had many intriguing life experiences. As a
young man, he was 'taught' the art of water dowsing.
During this dowsing experience, he became aware
that there are still many aspects of the natural world

we cannot explain. This awareness triggered an ongoing quest to find credible answers to his questions about life. He realised there is an intelligent 'life energy' at work in the material universe. This was the breakthrough that allowed him deep insights into the nature and origin of life on earth. These unique insights have been passed on in this book, offering a glimpse into the eternal nature of being, as well as where we've come from and where we might be going.

Enjoyed the book? You can follow Peter Griffiths at:

Website: www.petergriffithsauthor.com

Email: wearelife@petergriffithsauthor.com

9 780648 943